Lyrical Landscapes

10 EXPRESSIVE PIANO PIECES IN A VARIETY OF STYLES
MIKE SPRINGER

Foreword

Lyrical Landscapes, Book 1 is a collection of expressive pieces in a variety of styles and tempos. It was written to provide opportunities for late elementary to early intermediate students to develop skills in projecting lyrical, melodic lines. While many of the pieces were inspired by music from the Romantic era, lyric qualities are also applied to a variety of more contemporary styles.

From slow ballads to upbeat tempos, these pieces allow pianists the opportunity to develop a deeper musical awareness through the use of technical control, rubato, and subtle tempo changes. These pieces were composed so students not only enjoy performing the music, but grow musically along the way.

In memory of Olivia Joan Smith

Contents

Alfred

Alfred Music
P.O. Box 10003
Van Nuys, CA 91410-0003
alfred.com

ISBN-10: 1-4706-3896-7
ISBN-13: 978-1-4706-3896-2

Canyon Shadows

Mike Springer

Clear Mountain Sky

Mike Springer

Colors at Dawn

Mike Springer

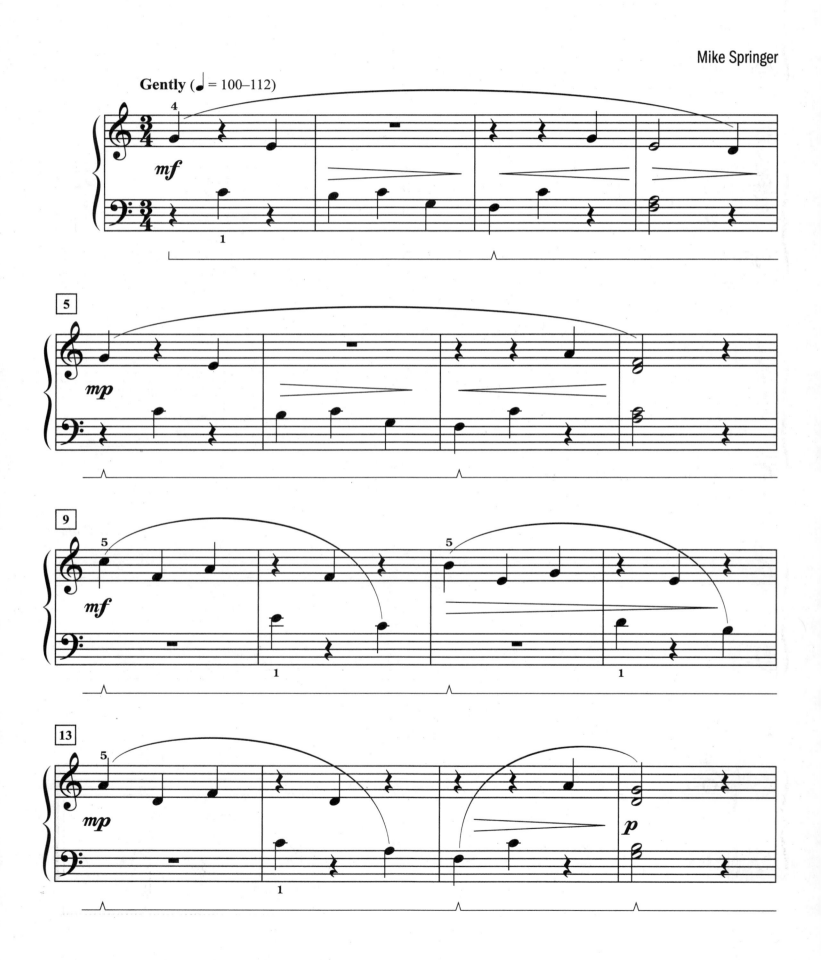

Floating on the Pond

Mike Springer

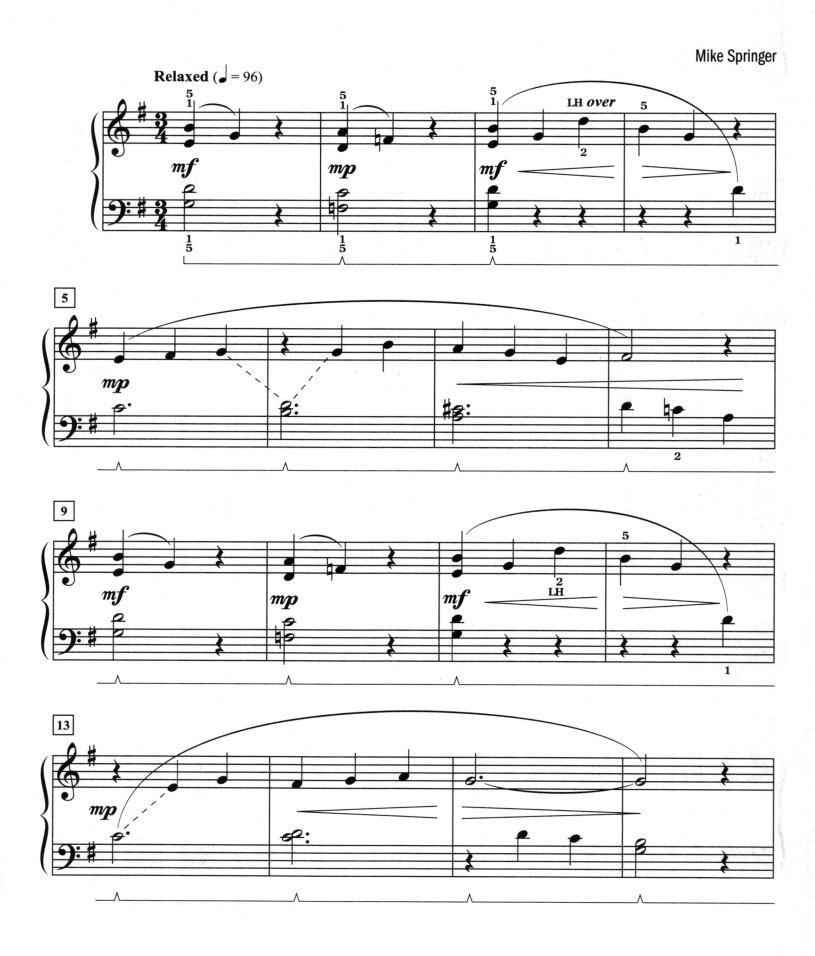

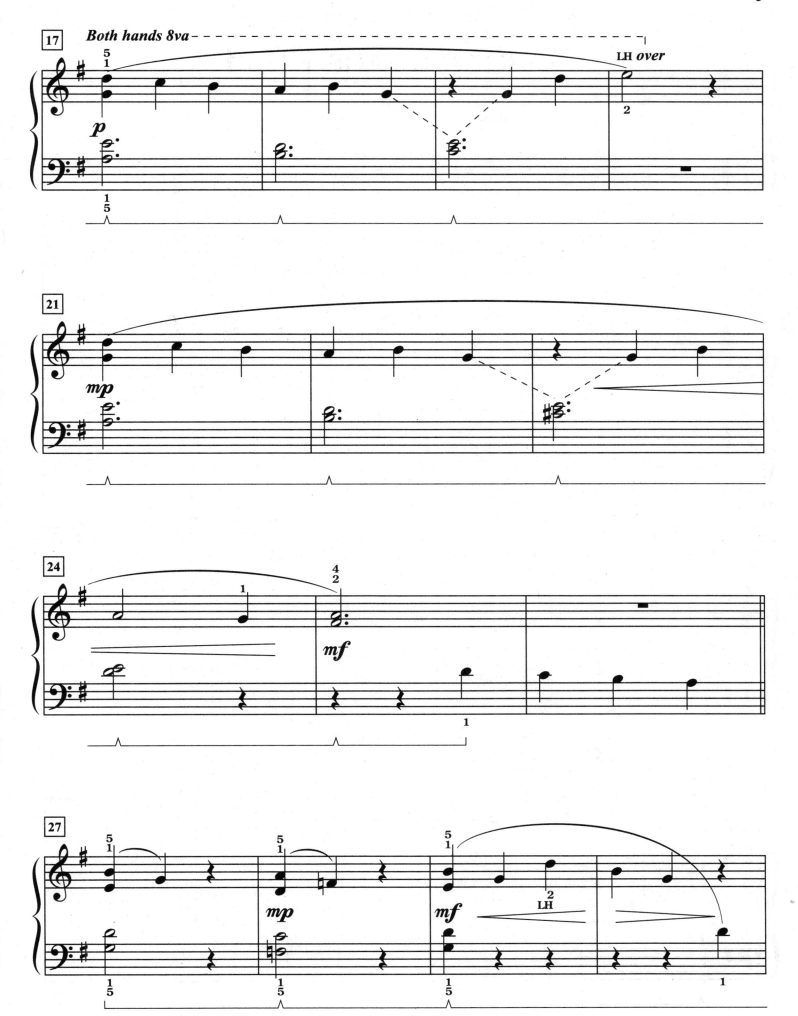

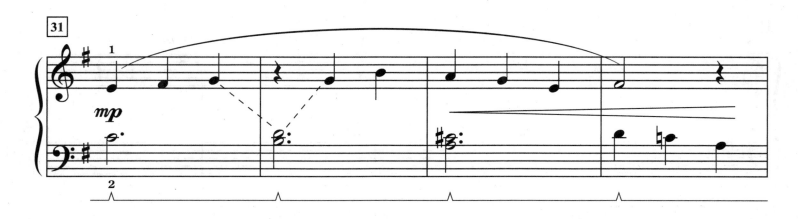

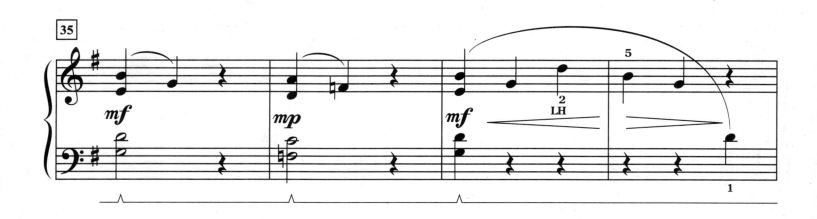

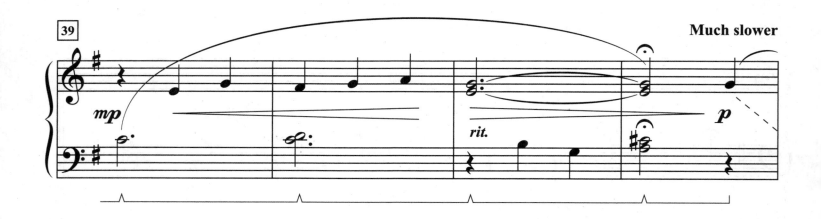

Fond Memories

Mike Springer

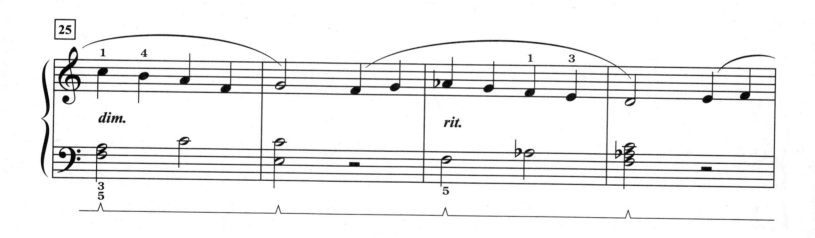

Gentle Rain

Mike Springer

Guarding the Castle Gates

Mike Springer

Il tenero fiore
(The Tender Flower)

Mike Springer

Sea Fog

Mike Springer

Quiet Moments

Mike Springer

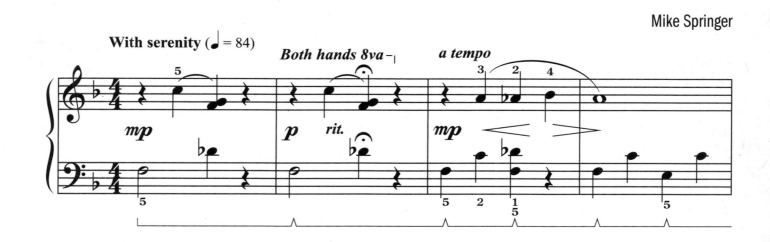

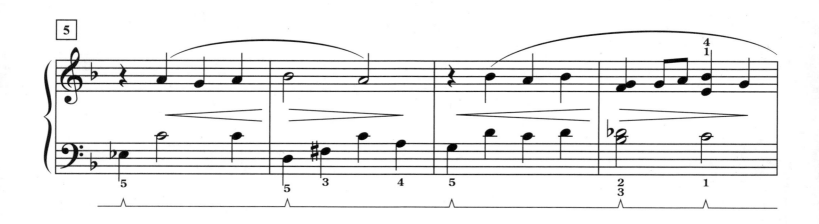

Slowly, with freedom

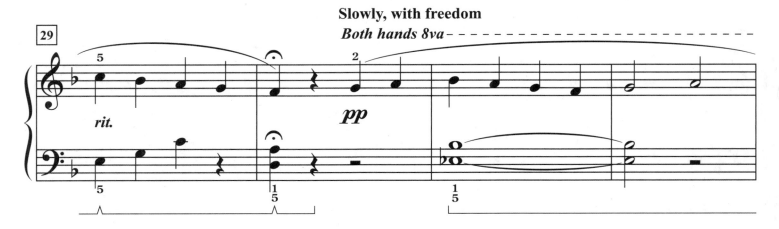

Tempo I

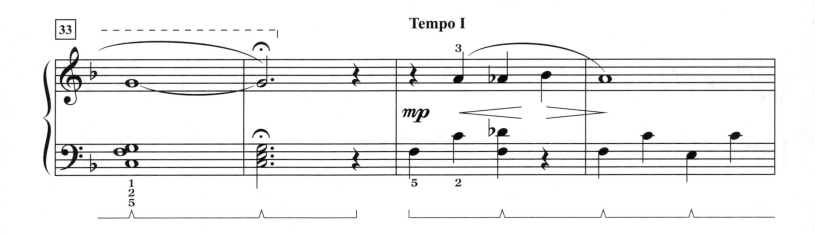

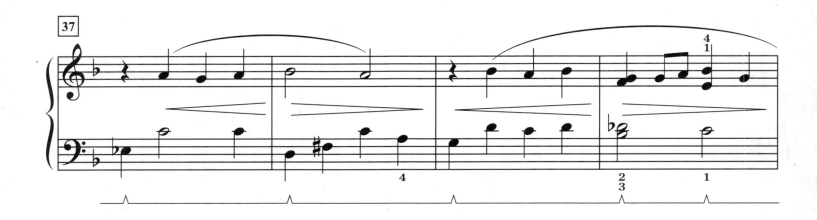

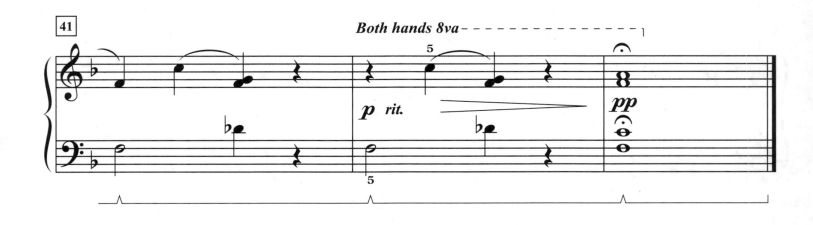